Manuela Zeitlhofer at minus 50 degrees Celsius (December 16, 2010)

Copyright © 2013 by Manuela Zeitlhofer.

All rights reserved. No part of this book may be reproduced or used in any manner whatsoever without the express written permission of the author except for the use of brief quotations in a book review.

Manuela Zeitlhofer
PO Box 742
Dawson City, YT, Canada Y0B 1G0

<zeitlhofer_manuela@yahoo.ca>

This book is available on *Amazon*: <www.amazon.com>, <www.amazon.ca> and on *Amazon* Europe.

Content

Our house (June 24, 2011)

About this book

We live amidst the untouched wilderness of the Yukon Territory in Canada, 120 kilometers north of Dawson City. Our property is located at the mouth of Poppy Creek on the Yukon River.

Our closest human neighbors live 30 kilometers away. Long, cold winters with little daylight dominate our life. The lack of modern amenities makes hard physical labor necessary. We spend a good part of our days carrying out tasks like getting firewood with a sled, hauling water in buckets, and cooking dinner without electricity or plumbing.

This book is based on the diary I kept for the first two years of my life in the wilderness. It documents a typical year, starting with spring: In late March nature is starting to awaken, the sun comes back, the river ice is about to break and after eight months of winter, travel by boat will soon be possible again.

Gaetan, Manuela and Lance (July 20, 2008)

The main characters

Gaetan Beaudet has been living in Poppy Creek long enough to become part of the land. Away from here he seems to lack part of himself. His spirit is connected with and nurtured by the pristine nature around us. Gaetan was born in Quebec. He moved up North in his late teens. After working in Dawson City for a few years, he decided to give away his car and purchase a boat with which he went downriver to find Poppy Creek. He built a cabin here and has been living in it for more than thirty years. Gaetan is an artist. He carves life sized birds out of wood.

Manuela Zeitlhofer: I was born in Austria and immigrated to Canada in 2003. To live in the untouched wilderness of the Canadian North has always been magically attractive for me. I used to be a sociologist, a teacher, and a tour guide, before I fell in love with Gaetan and Poppy Creek. In 2008, Lance and I moved here. I like to create practical leather garments, like mukluks, moccasins, gloves and mittens, using self-made patterns.

Lance is our dog. With some empathy we see the world through his eyes as a wonderful place full of exciting smells, and life as a constant adventure that should be enjoyed with total devotion. Lance and I found each other in a dog shelter in 2008, when he was only a few months old. Lance is a cross-breed and incorporates the best of Golden Lab, German Shepherd, Hound and possibly more.

Gaetan looking at the river (May 22, 2006)

Silence: Why I chose to live in the woods

By Gaetan

As a child I had a recurring dream: Frankenstein is chasing me (dragging foot and all) and eventually I am standing on the edge of a cliff, scared. I have two choices: I let him take hold of me or I jump. What do I have to lose? So I leap into the air arms out, expecting to fall like a rock but instead I am slowly floating like a feather and gently touching ground. I turn around, look up at my monster and laugh my head off as I walk away.

That's more or less how I felt 30 some years ago, when I quit my jobs and relationship, gave my car away, threw my belongings in my boat and left town on my way downriver and never looked back. It was either that or go insane. That first winter in the woods was the most memorable, magical experience in my life. And the following spring was like being born again.

Whether it's a week, a year, or a lifetime; I highly recommend it. Once you have mastered your restlessness and quiet down, you start to pay attention to details, to the relationship with each living thing you encounter. And when the duality you live in disappears (sooner or later it has to) you realize that you are IT. Appreciation and gratitude follow - that simple.

For the longest time I thought that the only way to achieve this understanding was being in a monastery in the Himalayas, but I was wrong: It can be done anywhere. It is all around us - to each his own. We are guided daily with songs, books, art, or a friend to make us understand. And once we do, it is just the beginning.

Gaetan goes for a winter walk (March 3, 2011)

Gaetan is stacking firewood (March 27, 2009)

Life in the wilderness: Somewhere between romantic and backbreaking

The myth is one of a warm cabin in a cold winter storm, of happy people sitting around the stove, and of warm summer days and romantic sunsets.

To convey the whole spectrum of pleasures and challenges this lifestyle implies, one has to understand that life happens between the romantic notion of fires crackling in the stove while the wind is howling at minus 40 degrees, and nature that imposes its laws on anybody alike: We have to be prepared for as many eventualities as possible and be aware of the dangers.

Hard physical work is necessary to meet our basic needs (for food, water and firewood for example) without much technology (other than a chain saw and a sled), while juggling the unforeseen (like forest fires or floods) and the unavoidable (like cold temperatures, wind, mosquitoes, things breaking and the scarcity of financial funds).

Modern amenities like running water, plumbing, electricity and road access are not existent at our home. Consequently, improvisation is the handiest skill to have or to acquire quickly as needed.

Why we do it anyways: Because we believe that this is the lifestyle that makes us happy, and even if our bodies are tired at night, our souls feel at rest.

The old cabin a few days before it was destroyed by the flood (May 3, 2009)

From oil lamps to satellite internet

When he first moved here in 1980, Gaetan owned one chainsaw and a 25-horsepower boat motor. For light, he used oil lamps and candles, and when he wanted to get to Dawson City during the winter, he had to walk and pull a sled. That took him several days each way.

Over the years, Gaetan acquired more tools (and even more spare parts), generators and motors. But he also gained the awareness that more is never enough. Therefore, he is cognizant of the energy we use. We try to conserve electricity, using LED lights, for example, and solar panels.

In 2009, I introduced satellite internet to Poppy Creek. This way, we are connected to the world, even though we are very far away from it at times. The discrepancy between the timeless wildness of the place we live at and the rapidly evolving technology we are using is something we muse about frequently. Mostly, we simply enjoy both though.

Poppy Creek from across the river (July 27, 2012)

A map of our property at Poppy Creek

Old cabin: Gaetan built it in 1980 and lived in it for almost 30 years. In 2009 it was flooded to the roof and has been uninhabitable since then. We use it as storage space now.

Studio / shop: Built in 2000, this building was used as rodent-proof storage room until I started utilizing it for my crafting projects during the winter of 2008/2009. From May 2009, after the flood had evicted us from the old cabin, until February 2010, Gaetan, Lance and I lived in it. Since then, Gaetan uses the studio as a carving shop.

New house: In the late 1990's, Gaetan had started to clear the land, collect building logs, and start to build this new, two-story cabin. After the flood in 2009, we finished the first section of it so we could move out of our exile, the studio. We have been living here since February 2010, enjoying how bright, warm and rodent-proof it is.

Cottage / guest cabin: We built this cabin in May 2009, because my mother had been invited and we had no other accommodation to offer. She was supposed to live in the studio, but the flood had changed our plan: We were evicted from the old cabin and moved into the studio. She was the first guest to accommodate the new guest cabin, lovingly referred to as "Mum's Cottage".

Additional buildings: Tool shed (built in 2003), bath house/sauna (built in 2007), two outhouses (one old, one built in 2011).

The map on the next page shows our property and the buildings on it on the confluence of Poppy Creek with the Yukon River (2013).

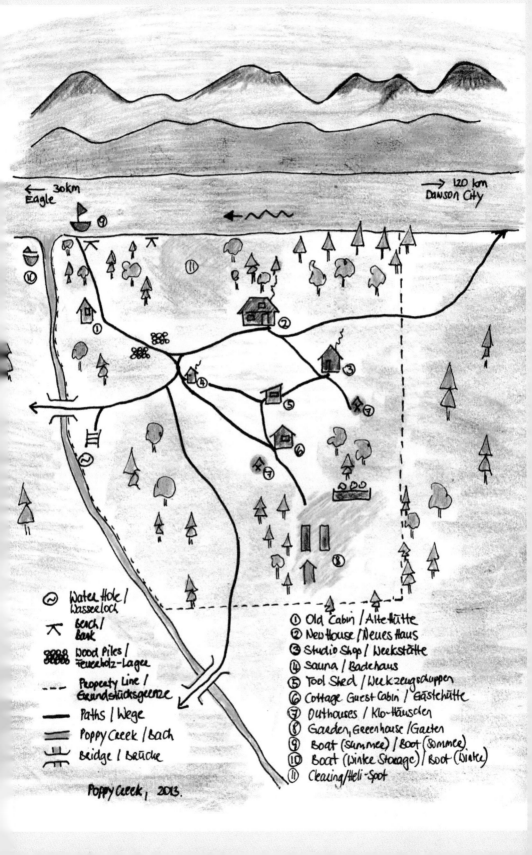

← 30km
Eagle

→ 120 km
Dawson City

Water Hole /
Wasserloch

Beach /
Bank

Wood Piles /
Feuerholz-Lager

Property Line /
Grundstücksgrenze

Paths / Wege

Poppy Creek / Bach

Bridge / Brücke

① Old Cabin / Alte Hütte
② New House / Neues Haus
③ Studio Shop / Werkstätte
④ Sauna / Badehaus
⑤ Tool Shed / Werkzeugschupper
⑥ Cottage Guest Cabin / Gästehütte
⑦ Outhouses / Klo-Häuschen
⑧ Garden, Greenhouse / Garten
⑨ Boat (Summer) / Boot (Sommer)
⑩ Boat (Winter Storage) / Boot (Winter)
⑪ Clearing / Heli-Spot

Poppy Creek, 2013.

Looking at the ice that is piled up to the top of the 12-meter high bank (May 3, 2009)

Spring

River breakup

Crocus with bee (May 2, 2009)

Bear tracks (July 19, 2010)

Sharing space
February 13

We are sharing the natural space around us with creatures, most of which we hardly ever see. However, we regularly see the tracks of wolves, lynx, fox, weasel, bear, and moose. Sometimes we also find caribou tracks. Smaller mammals and some birds are easier to spot. Especially in the summer we see bald eagles and peregrine falcons here. Ravens are always around. Squirrels, mice, and shrews can become annoying when they treat our food as theirs.

A few weeks ago, we found wolf tracks in the snow. One print was as big as the palm of my hand! We can expect to hear them howling any time of the year. Last spring, we counted a pack of 20 wolves walking on the far bank of the river.

So far I had three black bear encounters here in Poppy Creek: I met one bear on a hike about 500 meters from the house. The poor creature appeared to be at least as startled as I was and took off without a moment's hesitation. I had stopped, but honestly I had had no time to react in the fraction of a second that it took the bear to run off the other way!

The other two bears visited us by the cabin. One of them was especially persistent. I had just left the cabin when I noticed a black spot in the corner of my eyes. "A bear", I thought, and stepped back into the cabin. Gaetan came outside with me and we banged on tin cans to chase the animal away. The bear was not easy to irritate, though. Casually he climbed on the roof of the old sauna, where he started to chew on an ancient antler. I remember his eyes vividly: They were small, shiny, alert black dots that never let us out of sight. Gaetan fired a shotgun in the air. That did the trick. Finally the racket was too

Boreal chickadee (February 9, 2009)

much for him and he trotted off, slowly and in a self-confident manner. His backside, black and enormous was shifting with each step, while he disappeared into the forest.

In the winter, rabbit tracks can be found all around the property. We hardly ever see them though because they blend in so well with the snow. Also, evolution has taught them to be wary of predators, such as humans. Ravens flee too, but with more dignity, as if they made the conscious decision to leave the space to us. It is usually so quiet here that I can hear the dry rustling of their feathers when they flap their wings. Eagles generally remain in control of the situation. Usually they stay where they are when we spot them, quite frequently up on the top of a high tree on the riverbank, and they observe us attentively. The eye sight of an eagle is about 30 times better than that of a human!

Raven chicks (June 10, 2009)

Searching for signs of spring
April 13

It has been a long winter, and it seems to me as if plants, animals and humans alike are holding their breaths, expectantly searching for signs of the approaching spring. I took a closer look at birches, poplars, and highbush cranberry bushes and found that their buds are still small but shiny, colorful, and ready to explode into fresh green leaves as soon as the temperature warms up.

Our squirrel neighbours must have emptied their food caches, for they have been feeding on rose hips for the past week. They look skinny as they hop around on the hard snow and climb the bendable rose bushes.

I have been starting my garden plants. The new house offers plenty of light window sills for the project. I am looking forward to the first greens out in the wild - fireweed and yarrow sprouts - but it will be a few weeks before I can expect to pick them. Right now, the snow cover on the property is still up to 40 centimeters thick.

Gaetan uses what the season provides him with: enough snow to drive the snowmobile on. He has been hauling logs for firewood and lumber early in the day, when the trails are still hard enough to drive on. In the afternoons, he has been in the shop, working on his bird carvings.

Sheep Rock (May 22, 2010)

So beautiful, it almost hurts
April 19

We went on our first spring hike up Sheep Rock, a steep hill that overlooks several river bends. The following day we had an Easter picnic upriver. At a log jam with a great view of the mountains we started a fire, set up our picnic chairs and had our sandwiches. We savored the warmth of the sun, the hooting of owls and the sight of a graceful bald eagle. While we drove our snowmobile on the increasingly mushy trail, Lance enjoyed the run, but spent the rest of the afternoon napping.

The sunlight is orange now, not blue and cold like in the winter, when the sun lingers around the horizon. Things look golden and warm, even though the temperature remains around freezing. The snow is melting rapidly, exposing things I have not seen in half a year, like the fire pit and the forest ground!

The creek started overflowing several days ago. First, there was just more water, then, one day, I heard the water purling under the ice. The creek was awake again! By now there is a lot of water, flowing on top of and under the ice. It tastes a bit like moss and decaying leaves – the taste of forest. Inside, mosquitoes and flies wake up. The humming of their wings against the glass of the windows speaks of summer, and memories of spruce resin frying in the sun tickle my nose.

Our days are full: I just finished a set of curtains for the cabin windows. For holdings I used burl wood that we found at one of our firewood sites. Gaetan uses the warmer days for maintenance and repair work. He has also started to cut lumber. The receding snow levels make a yard clean up possible.

Lance by the river bank in the early morning (April 19, 2010)

Landlocked: Breakup season started
April 20

Last night a small section of the river channel opened up below Poppy Creek. Warm, sunny days, rapidly melting snow and overflowing water on top of the river ice announce the end of our winter. Soon, the river will be free of ice, marking the beginning of summer. Sometime between the end of April and mid-May we will experience a few glorious days of spring: Seemingly every plant will awaken at the same time and the calls of countless migratory birds will fill the air. But I am getting ahead of things.

The river ice is bare of snow. Because of the darker water underneath, the clear ice absorbs more sunlight which increases the speed the ice is melting at. Big puddles of water and soggy snow along the shores of the river make it impossible to use the snowmobile. We are landlocked until mid-May when river travel by boat will be possible again.

Ice-channel in the creek (April 20, 2010): I filter my drinking water by means of a micro-filter. Gaetan drinks it untreated.

Creek picking up flavors
April 22

Every morning I walk to the creek and haul water back to the house. We use four 20-liter buckets with lids that screw on to keep the water from spilling out. During the past few days, the color of our water changed from crystal clear to light brown. The taste evolved from lively to cool with an earthy undertone. The temperatures have been well above freezing during the day. In addition, it rained last night. The creek was asleep for half a year. Now it is awake and eager to move. The water has carved an impressive, 40-centimeter wide channel into the two-meter thick ice.

At the mouth of the creek and along the river shore, water is overflowing. More and more melt water is pushing up the ice cover on the Yukon River. The first ducks are landing along the open water.

Along the shores we spotted caribou tracks. As far as we could tell, the animals crossed the river.

Mouse visiting compost (September 4, 2011)

And what are we doing?
April 22

Gaetan declared the woodcutting season to be over and stored the snowmobiles away for the summer. He takes the foam seats off, because bears like to take probing bites out of them, empties the gas tanks and puts the track on blocks of wood so they remain off the ground. Then he covers the vehicles up with tarps.

Yesterday, with birds chirping and water dripping under the sun's warming rays, Gaetan did some laundry outside. In the winter, we do all our laundry by hand and mostly inside. Due to the lack of indoor plumbing we only use the washing machine outside and during the summer.

In the meantime, I built a compost frame. It can be quite challenging to obtain fertile soil from compostable plant-components. For one, we are confronted with a short growing season and a consequently sun-deprived, cool, and arid climate. In addition, our compost used to have no time to decompose before Lance came along and ate everything that has any nutritional value (a dog's digestive system is very resilient, it seems!). And finally, squirrels, birds and mice devoured the remains of vegetables and fruit routinely.

The way I am dealing with the first challenge is by making compost piles on which I grow cucumbers and zucchinis: The humidity accelerates decomposition and the resulting warmth benefits the plants. Lance, as well as squirrels and birds I have managed to keep (partly) out of the compost by constructing compost frames. But mice will just have to be endured – a small price to pay for the pleasure of knowing them outside!

Caribous 400 meters away (April 22, 2010)

17 Caribous crossing the river
April 23

It was around midday, when I walked to the river bank to look out for Gaetan and Lance who had left for a walk after breakfast. My eyes wandered over the frozen river, when I caught sight of a group of caribous on the island out front.

It is hard to describe my excitement: I have never seen more than two caribous at a time around here, and there were 10 animals slowly walking along, looking out for a way to cross the river. Quickly, I took a few pictures, before I realized that this time, my pocket camera would not be sufficient. I raced back to the house and hauled Gaetan's Nikon-on-a-tripod back to the river bank.

I stood in awe, witnessing the animals marching slowly from their winter feeding grounds to their spring calving grounds. The females will give birth soon. Last year's calves were still nursing or trying to, I could not tell. They survived a long cold winter, the constant presence of predators, scarcity of food supplies, maggots in their skin, and the crossing of ice cold rivers. What really got to me though was the realization that none of these natural aspects of their habitat could do as much harm to them as my species has been doing to theirs: Over the last 150 years, humans have reduced the size of local caribou herds to

Caribous marching slowly across the frozen river (April 22, 2010)

a fraction of their original size. 70 years ago, stern-wheeler boats had to stop to give way to thousands of animals crossing the river. Even Gaetan in his 30 years here has witnessed hundreds of caribous walking through the property!

From a caribou's perspective, the day was probably relatively unspectacular:

I did not sleep much last night (as usual). Others kept watch. There was not much food around for breakfast, so we decided to cross the river. The first part was easy and we reached the island without getting our hooves wet. Then we crossed open water. The young ones struggled to get back out onto the ice. Two lead animals tried to cross the second channel, but could not get out on the other side (too much current), so they turned around and we camped on the ice for a few hours. Rest was much needed. The young ones were hungry, so we moved on in the late afternoon. Food has yet to be found.

When those 10 animals settled down to rest, we (Gaetan had come home in the meantime) spotted another group of 7 caribous as they were crossing the river further down. They were successful and disappeared into the forest. We left our observation point and had a late lunch. After that we went back in regular intervals to check on the campers. At one point they were gone.

Wolf in the middle of the river (April 25, 2009)

Talk with a wolf
April 26

Ten minutes ago I was reading in bed, when I heard wolves howling. Within a few minutes I headed down the path to the river. It is so exciting to see these creatures around. They represent freedom and grace for me. Now I am standing on top of the steep river bank. In one hand I am holding the pocket camera, and with the other hand I protect my eyes from the brightness of the sun that has just risen above the horizon.

Five wolves are on their way downriver. Up until two minutes ago all of them were on the other side of the river, 500 meters away from me. Then the last one in the row suddenly turned left and started to run toward me. Blinded by the sun I did not realize what was going on at first. Then the dot with four legs grew bigger.

I have been waiting for what is going to happen since then. When the wolf is halfway across the river, Lance comes bouncing down the trail. I turn my head to him and whisper "stay". Obediently he sits down and waits, and I congratulate myself for the efforts I have been putting into his training.

Something on this side of the river must have caught the wolf's curiosity, because he keeps moving away from the pack. I begin to take pictures. The wolf is only 100 meters away now, and still he keeps moving straight toward me. When he is only 50 meters away he turns to his right and away from me. He stops again and turns around to look right in my eyes. I say "Hello wolf". He makes a leap forward before he stops again and looks back at me. I just stare at him. Then he starts running downriver. The other wolves are waiting for him. A few minutes later he is back with his pack.

Yukon River ice-free again! (April 28, 2010)

Breakup!
April 29

Two days ago, it was late in the afternoon and I was watering plants, when Gaetan pointed out that something was going on with the river. I looked out the window, and the ice on our side of the river was moving. Big sheets were slowly drifting by. We could even see some old snowmobile-tracks on the ice! For a moment, I could not tell whether it was the ice that was moving or the shore with me on it!

For about 24 hours, we had an open channel with smooth water in front of our place, but we could see solid ice upriver and downriver (downriver, ice had piled up on top of the still anchored ice-cover). Then, yesterday evening, something happened again: I had stepped outside to serve dinner to Lance, when I heard a deep rumbling, somehow resembling a distant thunder, accompanied by a vibration that I could feel in my core. Lance was startled too, and we both headed to the river and saw when the ice from the far side of the river slowly started to move.

It took two days before the river was open and flowing again. Ice kept floating by for a week and the air was cooler and more humid than before. What a gentle breakup it was compared to 2009, when the Yukon River had flooded our property. The old cabin we were living in at the time was flooded to the roof and uninhabitable afterward. We lost a lot of our belongings, like books, clothes, furniture, food, electric household appliances and tools. Clean-up took us a long time that summer. We stayed in the studio, a 4x5 meter big, one-room cabin, and worked on the new house, so we could move in as soon as possible.

Moose (June 5, 2009)

Moose visit
May 1

It is half past noon. I am walking to the studio, when I see something from the corner of my eyes. I turn my head and my brain announces "Horse – no, we do not have horses here! Moose!" The next moment I start rushing back to the cabin to inform Gaetan and grab my camera. "Moose on the clearing by the river!" A few years back, Gaetan had cleared a piece of forest, so a helicopter could land in case of an emergency. The former woods are now a grassy field with willows sprouting - a delicacy for a moose!

I rush back out and watch the moose meander with long, elastic steps behind the studio and over to the creek, where he turns around and disappears into the forest upriver. I follow the tracks for a while before I decide it is time to let him go: He visited and now he is on his way again.

Grey jay bathing in the sun (May 8, 2010)

Good and bad?

May 9

Is there good and bad in nature? Life and death, can we line them up against each other, or are they part of the same thing, part of the circle of life?

Here is the story: Yesterday morning, Gaetan went for a walk. He assumed there might be an animal carcass upriver, since he had observed raven, gulls and eagles circling in the air. When he came back, he reported a caribou carcass just upriver from our trail entrance. The animal had probably died during breakup (and we thought it was a smooth breakup!). Maybe it had been pushed under the ice while crossing an open section, maybe it had tried to cross the river and broke through the ice, maybe it had been caught on a drifting ice sheet. We do not know. All we know is the end of the story. The caribou is now food for other animals. Ravens for example are feeding their young with the meat. And life goes on. Still, it is hard to see beyond death.

In the afternoon, I was still dwelling on the caribou's destiny while I was working in the back garden, when two grey jays dropped in to take a sunbath in dry leaves. I sat down and watched them. They were all fluffed up. Such pleasure, such enjoyment, such devotion! I am still smiling as I put the experience in words.

Later that day, everything started to make sense for me, and I found comfort in the fact that life and death need each other. We either accept them both, or we lose much zest for life, I believe.

Black bear by the river (May 17, 2010)

Big game abundance
May 18

I feel like I am in a big game park. It seems that whenever we step outside we see some big mammal or tracks thereof:

A big black bear was visiting our back yard. Later, I went for a walk and ran into him again. So I turned around and walked the other way and there were fresh moose tracks.

We went on a boat ride a day later, and saw a small black bear on an island. Minutes later, a caribou bounced along the shoreline. His antlers were freshly growing, covered in smooth velvet. He ran with a bit of a kick in every step, carrying his tail up, showing the white patch underneath. We stopped the boat to go for a walk and there were grizzly tracks! On the way home we saw two moose and another black bear.

Food scarcity in May
May 18

The last time I bought food was in late March. Now, we are out of most store-bought fresh food that keeps well, like potatoes, onions, garlic, cabbage, eggs and apples. All we have left for fresh food are some carrots, supplemented with fireweed and yarrow shoots from the yard. Cooking becomes challenging if all you have are canned and pickled things and dry food. To take a five hour trip into town just for food is not easy to justify either, and since we are waiting for some things to get sorted out first, we are postponing our shopping trip for the time being.

Boat on dry ground (May 18, 2009)

Story about a flood and a boat
May 20

Not so long ago there was a place somewhere in the bush, somewhere in a country not so far away. That place was quiet and peaceful for most of the year. Two people and one dog were living amongst their wild neighbors. One day in early spring news arrived that there would be a flood. The animals of the forest and the dog started to move to higher ground, and the two people started to move their belongings to higher ground.

On the third day of their exodus the water started to rise beyond the wildest imaginations of the two people. The animals were still unimpressed and just kept moving uphill. The people took their boat, one of their most valuable possessions, and kept pulling it to the edge of the water, as the water was rising.

On the evening of the fourth day the water started to recede, and the wild animals came back down to lower grounds. The two people, however, found that much of their belongings were still on higher ground: Their freezer was nestled into moss, their spare boat motor was tied to a tree, along with a propane bottle and a barrel of fuel. And their boat was now on dry ground 300 meters from the river, amidst the forest. Let me tell you, the trees were startled, and it takes a lot to startle a tree!

The people were busy with their dwelling and the things therein for two weeks. Then they decided that it was time to ease the tensions that had arisen amongst the trees and pull the boat back to where it belonged – into the river. It took one of them three days to accomplish the goal, but then it was done.

Everything was again the way it was supposed to be: The wild animals were doing the wild thing, the dog was doing the dog thing, the trees were doing the tree thing (with their roots in the dirt and their trunks in the air instead of in the water), the boat was back in the water, the water was back in its original bed, and the people occupied themselves with some of their other belongings. And life went on as usual.

Crocuses on the hill (May 3, 2009)

Days like warm honey
May 24

We are in between seasons right now. It is hot like in the summer, but we have no mosquitoes and no smoke from wildfires yet. The last few days have been a gift with clear sky, a few clouds here and there, amazing sweet smells from blooming poplars and birches, a soft breeze, and literally two mosquitoes (they were successfully repelled by my threats to kill them upon a second encounter with my skin). I have been wearing shorts and a T-shirt all afternoon!

Still snow on the mountain tops (May 16, 2010)

Gaetan and Lance arriving by boat to pick me up at Forty Mile (May 26, 2009)

24 hours in Dawson City
May 27

We really needed fresh food and mail had accumulated in the past months, so I caught a ride into Dawson City with our neighbors, for a day and a half.

On the way there, we spent four hours on the boat and my face got sun burnt. I spent the night with friends, their two children, a cat, and a dog. The next morning, I took care of the mail, ran tons of errands, went grocery shopping and was engaged in a number of conversations by people I know.

On the way back, we drove the first half of the way via car. It was a good thing I had not bought any eggs. They would not have done so well on the brisk ride on gravel roads with potholes. Gaetan then picked me up at the boat landing in Forty Mile, and we covered the remaining 40 kilometers by boat.

It was so wonderful to be back home!

Raining cloud (May 17, 2010)

Spring rain
May 29

It had become very dry over the past weeks. Gaetan therefore installed a sprinkler system. The Yukon Territory is generally arid during the summer, and forest fires are a natural part of our forest's life cycle.

When I was in Dawson a few days ago, the "water bomber" (a plane equipped with water tanks) was already busy extinguishing a fire somewhere around Dawson. The forest fire we had in Poppy Creek four years ago stopped just a few hundred meters away from the buildings. The fire department provided us with a heavy duty water pump and a sprinkler system.

Fortunately we got a nice thunder shower two days ago, and last night it drizzled for several hours: warm, soft spring rain! This morning the sky was still cloudy. It is wonderful that all the mud that was left behind by the high water during breakup finally gets washed away!

Two birds of a feather (June 1, 2009)

Birds' offspring
May 30

Our juvenile neighbors remain a source of delight. Yesterday I got the chance to save the life of one of them. He or she had fallen into a half full water bucket: While I was busy feeding the other birds, I heard wings splashing in the water and banging on the bucket. Quickly I was at the scene and carefully grabbed the animal with both hands. The unlucky bird was fully drenched. I put him on the ground and immediately he started to shake and fluff up his feathers. He hopped over to a tree and managed a jump-flight onto the lowest branch. The next ten minutes were spent reorganizing and drying his plumage.

Gaetan's heart belongs to the birds: His face lightens up when they are around. Yesterday, when he was working on the roof of the tool shed, the grey jay chicks came along. I brought him some pancake and he fed them, and that's when everything about him seemed to make sense again.

Many young grey jays will be killed by predatory birds this summer. One of the four juvenile birds will hopefully survive to spend the winter with its parents.

Enjoying the view (July 12, 2009)

Summer

Garden - Contracting Work - Building Projects - Visitors

Fireweed in full bloom on top of the steep river bank (July 15, 2009)

Raised bed near old cabin (June 21, 2009)

Finally: Gardens fully operational!
June 1

As of today, all my gardens are fully operational. The nights are still chilly, but the days warm up to 25 degrees.

I have a garden by the old cabin, close to the bank of the creek, and another one behind the guest cabin. Over the years I have narrowed down the plant species that thrive here in rather acidic soil, with not too much sun (even in our sunniest spot we only get the sun for 8 hours at the high of summer, but daylight for up to 22 hours) and a short growing season (June, July and August are mostly frost free). The raised bed in my "creek garden" hosts plants that like the more humid location in partial shade: peas and beans, chives, salads and kale. The new garden lies in our sunniest spot and harbors the greenhouse as well as several raised beds: Tomatoes and cucumbers thrive in the greenhouse. Squashes, zucchini, rhubarb and herbs grow on the raised beds.

I hope there are no seed eating birds in the area. There IS a suspect: Yesterday I saw a thrush (I believe a Swanson's thrush) four times in or around the raised bed. Gaetan advocates for it, telling me that that particular bird does not feed off seeds, but off ants and other insects. We will see!

Furthermore I hope that the hares won't find my salad, but onions planted amongst the lettuce will hopefully keep those fellows away from my "grass"!

Doing laundry amongst trees
June 2

We inherited an old washing machine that had survived the flood in 2009. Since we do not have a room with plumbing, the machine has to stay outside for the time being. Set up on the side of the porch, we used it for the first time today. It was a hot day, and even in the shade I could smell hot spruce resin. Doing laundry was a very pleasant and relaxing, albeit hot, experience.

Gaetan inspected my operation and commented: "It is by all means not a beauty, but it works!" Then he set up laundry lines amongst the trees for me, before he went back to his work. I had to carry buckets of water from the rainwater tank to the washing machine, add detergent (we use only fully bio-degradable laundry soap, by the way), the laundry and wait while the machine, operated by our generator did the washing. After that, I stopped the washer, wrung out the first set of laundry and put it in a bucket where it had to await the rinsing cycle, while I did another load or two of darker and dirtier laundry in the same water. The same process had to be repeated for the rinsing cycle. Then I hung my fresh clean sheets and clothes amongst the trees.

Laundry drying amongst the trees (May 18, 2009)

34

New photo-voltaic panels on top of the studio roof (June 1, 2009)

Gaetan's projects
June 3

Gaetan has been working on his projects for the past weeks, but I was too busy to document his progress:

The new photo-voltaic panels are installed on top of the studio roof. They are wired to the battery system, which is located on the porch. Included in that system are the generator and the satellite internet system: Lots of wires that speak a language I do not understand.

The tool shed, which was used as an unstructured storage space is now equipped with a workbench and shelves. Even I will be able to find my way around in there. The boat and the motors have been serviced and are working reliably.

Gaetan also started to build a new guest cabin. I took on the role as a carpentry apprentice, which left me sore after carrying lumber from the piles to the building site.

The porcupine looked like a queen with her paw up on that stomp and her silver mane floating around her! (June 7, 2009)

Prickly transient
June 8

It was early evening and I was pushing the wheelbarrow back to the house when I heard Lance barking. He does not bark unless there is something to tell. The barking sounded serious. Then, only seconds later, another bark, and then another. I abandoned my wheelbarrow and started running toward the noise. Gaetan was already at the site with Lance seeking protection behind his legs.

Protection from what, I wondered, when I spotted the porcupine, facing a tree while slapping its prickly tail onto the ground toward us. Anybody who comes too close to a porcupine has to be ready to end up with quills in their own bodies. Yukon dogs are very much at risk for that kind of accident, even if it is just curiosity that motivates them to approach a porcupine. Anyway, Lance chose the safe thing to do: report and hide. As we took turns photographing the animal, Lance was leaning against the other person's knees. I could read his thoughts: "Quite fishy, that big thing!"

Sea of roses
June 12

Wherever we look we see wild roses in full bloom. Their sweet smell is lingering in the air. All these plants started to bloom on the same day, as if to make up for the thorns we have been, and will be ending up with in our skin all year round. After some time, my nose – regrettably - gets immune to the smell though.

Under the canopy of roses, blue bells, poppies, lady slippers and dogwood are opening their flowers as well.

Planning ahead
July 30

Summer is past its prime and more and more we are finding ourselves involved in discussions about what we need for the long winter ahead and how, where and when we are going to haul it in. The big things are building supplies for the new house, gas (we transport it in barrels) for snowmobiles, chainsaws, the boat and generators, and propane for cooking and lights.

In mid-October we will go on a last trip to Dawson to stock up on food for the winter (fresh vegetables and fruit, as well as canned and dry food). Food is my domain. Since we cannot go shopping - not even receive food in the mail from October to December - and since anything we bring in from then on until March might freeze during the haul, I need to plan now for what we will need for more than half a year.

The past few days the temperatures have been above 30 degrees Celsius. In addition, smoke from wildfires obscured the view of the mountains. It is hard for me to anticipate what I will need for seven cold winter months, while I am trying to stay out of the summer heat.

Gaetan offered some thoughts about his planning efforts, when it comes to tools and machines: "If you can anticipate what's going to break down, you can buy the parts in advance. But that's hard, and that's why you have two, three things of the same kind. If you have food, shelter and clothing, and if there is a problem with equipment, it's not a life-threatening situation, just a slow-down. Usually by December we are settled in our routines and can figure out what will be needed a few months down the road. Until mid-April we have the chance to haul things in by snowmobile. Then we have to get ready for breakup. For three to five weeks we cannot go anywhere. In any case, we don't feel like going anywhere because it is so beautiful here".

Double rainbow over Poppy Creek
August 3

After a night spiked with glaring lightning, rolling thunder and pouring rain, we went to check the fish wheel at six in the morning. It was still drizzling. Tattered storm clouds were scattered across the sky and another wall of grey rain was approaching from downriver. The world around us was wreathed in orange mist. When we arrived at the wheel, we looked back over to the house: The sun had just come over the horizon behind us, dipping the tops of the hills around Poppy Creek in orange light, and a double rainbow framed the scene.

Photo (next page): Rainbow (August 3, 2010)

Fishwheel in service (July 24, 2010): Fishwheels, propelled by the river's current were traditionally used to catch migrating salmon. This wheel consists of two pontoons, two baskets, two paddles and two holding tanks that are in the water to keep the fish alive.

Not enough time: Summer job, visitors and building projects
July & August

Summer job. In July and August of 2010, 2011 and 2012, we operated a catch-and-release fishwheel on the Yukon River close to our home. Our mandate was to collect data about Chinook salmon and report it to the Department of Fisheries and Oceans Canada. Based on that information, management decisions about fish harvest were made. The project has come to an end though.

Visitors. Summer is also the time when people visit the Yukon Territory. Especially my family and friends from Europe have been visiting us every summer so far.

Building projects. In 2009, we had to build a new guest cabin, since we had moved into the existing guest cabin after the flood and were expecting my mother to visit us. All that summer and well into the winter we also worked on a section of the new house. In 2010, we worked on smaller projects in and around the house. The summer of 2011 was dominated by Anya's arrival in June. While I was getting used to being a mother, Gaetan built a storage shed that is attached to the north side of the house. In 2012, he constructed a porch on two sides of the house from the main entrance to the storage room.

Summer is short as it is, and with these activities going on it feels even shorter.

Improvised fish-smoking device (July 25, 2009)

Improvisation: Learning about smoking fish

August 5

Yesterday, we received a trout from visitors. The information I had about smoking fish was scarce: Use alder wood, don't put the grill too close to the fire. The fish had come as a surprise, and so I did not have time to build a more permanent smoking device. I decided to start a small fire on the shore of the river. Pieces of tin metal served as siding and cover for my primitive smoking device.

Later that evening, when we saw aircraft carriers and gigantic helicopters on a movie, I found myself wondering if we are really living in the same world: We improvise with simple means, while somewhere out there people construct intricate technical devices.

Leaving those thoughts aside, the fish (even though more cooked than smoked) was delicious with garden salads and rice on the side. I will have to continue my fish smoking with local fish like arctic grayling, pike or burbot. Even though Chinook and Chum salmon are migrating up the Yukon River to reach their spawning grounds at its tributaries, there is a ban on salmon fishing in the Yukon again this summer, due to dwindling numbers of these animals.

Bear visit (August 5, 2009)

Bear visit
August 6

The tips of the dense black fur on his back are golden, as if bleached by the sun. His gait is leisurely and deliberate; his hips are slowly swaying left-right. His big paws do not make a sound as he is moving over the soft forest ground. His eyes are small, black, shiny and alert, with the gaze slightly out of focus. His ears, round and erect, are moving slightly as they scan his surroundings.

We had a black bear visitor last night! Judging by his size he was between two and three years old. He was strolling toward our studio-window when Gaetan spotted him: "Psst, come over quickly and see!" By then the bear was only ten meters from the window. I had a chance to take a few pictures, before the animal disappeared behind the corner of the cabin.

When we opened the front door, he turned his head, stopped for a second, and then ran away, not in panic, but as if motivated by a conscious decision: "I give way, because I choose so". Gaetan commented "That's a boy!" and I exclaimed "Good bear", expressing our mutual relief that brother bear had not been interested in our human settlement, but merely been traveling through.

Mouth of the creek washed out into the river (August 14, 2010)

Mud meets silt

August 7

Yesterday, for the second time in three weeks, we experienced torrential rain that lasted more than a day. Within hours, the creek rose rapidly. The river followed soon thereafter. Our second bridge across the creek was destroyed by the water. We had to evacuate all our belongings from the beach.

This morning it cleared up. Still, lots of driftwood is coming down the river, along with the occasional treasure (we harvested an empty jerry can, a piece of plywood and a broken plastic container). When I went up the creek this morning, Lance caught up with me just as I had reached the creek where the bridge had been. In his usual manner, he was bolting past me. Too late he realized that the bridge was gone, and in the blink of an eye he made up his mind (I could hear his thoughts: "I have to stop! No, I cannot stop! Oh no! I have to jump!") and tried to jump across the creek. He landed in the middle of it. Luckily, the creek had already slowed down, carrying less water. Had Lance attempted his stunt yesterday, he might have been swept away.

While the creek is usually clear, the river carries lots of glacial silt until late fall. With all that rain, the creek picked up rocks, sand, trees and dirt. Some creeks carried a lot of gravel that washed into the river like alluvial fans. Also, a vast number of landslides can be found along the river.

Eddy in front of Poppy Creek (October 12, 2008)

Fall

Harvesting - Hunting - Storing Supplies

Fall colors along the river (September 12, 2009)

Wild chives (June 18, 2008)

Harvesting-season started
August 8

Ever since the radishes sprouted, we have been snacking on the fruits of our garden: We savor salad, kale, peas, broccoli, herbs, rhubarb, zucchinis, and carrots as side dishes or as garnish on sandwiches.

About two weeks ago the raspberry season started. First, I snatched a few berries here and there, but during the last few days the ripe fruits have become too abundant to be eaten right there! When I ended up with three cups of raspberries, I blended them with an equal amount of rhubarb and made preserve. We do not have a fridge or freezer, so we have to take care of ripe fruits and vegetables in different ways, such as canning or drying them. My intention for that preserve was to use it as bread spreads, but it did not jell, so we will eat it as compote on one of those cold winter nights.

Yesterday, I also picked my first lowbush cranberries along the trails around the cabins. They are not fully ripe yet, but if I leave them we will step on and destroy them, or animals will harvest them: While worms are my main competitors for raspberries, it is mice who are feeding on lowbush cranberries. Lowbush cranberries ripen in a basket, even if they are left unrefrigerated.

Hardly worth mentioning for quantity, but so memorable for their flavor are currants: Both red and black currants can be found along the creek. It took me about an hour to pick two cups of them. I ate one cup and now I find myself wondering what I can do with one cup of those precious, aromatic berries.

Photos (next page): Lowbush cranberries, raspberries, zucchini, black currants, broccoli, highbush cranberries

Lance by the river bank (September 4, 2009)

We can see clearly again!
August 11

Finally, after more than a week during which we could sometimes not see 500 meters to the other side of the river, we enjoyed a wonderfully clear sunrise today. The mountains appeared blue in the morning light, sharply outlined in front of the cerulean sky. The thermometer showed plus two degrees Celsius (my poor garden plants!), and Gaetan started a fire in the kitchen stove shortly after six in the morning.

The smoke that had obstructed our view came from different wildfires in a radius of several hundred kilometers. When human settlements are not at risk, the authorities limit their actions to monitoring the fires. That makes sense, since wildfires are a natural part of the life cycle of forests. Fires also reduce the numbers of insects such as spruce beetles. In areas where wildfires have been controlled for several years, for example in Kluane National Park in the Southwest of the Yukon Territory, spruce beetles are destroying vast areas of forest. Where humans are interfering with natural cycles...

Mouth of Poppy Creek, Yukon River, and mountains in the background
(August 18, 2009)

Going for a walk
August 18

We have been enjoying two magnificent sunny fall days. After heavy rain showers during the night, the air is fresh and humid, a thin layer of fog hovers over the trees, the ground smells musty like mushrooms and moss, the first leaves are changing their colors, and the berries are ripening and contribute to the array of fall colors.

Yesterday morning I went to the next creek to pick cranberries. On the way back I found a dead juvenile peregrine falcon on the beach, hidden partially behind a piece of driftwood. The bird looked perfectly undamaged. Before I touched it, I poked it gently with a stick to make sure it was dead. When I picked it up the feathers rustled. What a beautiful bird!

Later we mused what it had died from: Did it break its neck while chasing some other bird or was it chased himself? It is sad, and it is hard for me to accept death as part of life.

New outhouse
August 19

August 18, 2009. I decided to start digging a hole for a new outhouse. The old one is close to the old cabin and too far from both the new house and the studio. Despite my elbow, which is not used to all the lifting, the hole was growing quickly. In less than two hours I had dug hip deep, and one by one meters wide.

August / September 2009. I kept digging for several more days, until the hole was as deep as I am tall (which is 170 centimeters), and I needed a ladder to get out of the hole. Gaetan said it was not deep enough. I replied that I could not possibly dig any deeper. The project laid dormant (and covered with a sheet of plywood) for the winter.

August 16, 2010. Gaetan dug another 30 centimeters before we moved the outhouse building on top of the hole by means of a winch. Finally, we had a new view!

The hole (August 17, 2009)

Outhouse in its new location
(August 16, 2010)

Busy fall days
August 25

The world around us is changing rapidly. So much is happening in nature! Right now, at seven in the morning, I am looking out the window into twilight. I saw the stars again last night after almost half a year during which the nights were never dark. The days are getting shorter quickly: The sun is rising around seven now. Only a few weeks ago it rose at six.

Leaves are changing color, some are already falling off. The days are rainy. The nights are colder, leaving me worried about my fragile greens, especially the tomatoes that are slow to ripen. The indigenous inhabitants of our plant world on the other hand are flourishing: Highbush cranberries and rosehips are abundant, and we found humongous mushrooms.

Flocks of sandhill cranes and Canada geese are moving south. Their calls, together with the humid smells of the forest put me in a fall mood.

What I did the last few days:
• Harvested herbs, built a drying rack, dried herbs by the stove
• Picked berries
• Canned zucchini, made rose hip jelly and cranberry juice
• Cut my hair

We have been ordering all kinds of things for the building project and supplies for the winter, such as tools, a 12-volt-ceiling fan and a stove-top fan, a vacuum cleaner and food. The rain keeps delaying the completion of some of our outdoor endeavors. It is hard to explain the intricate connections between tasks and how the delay of one causes a chain reaction for a seemingly infinite number of others.

What we still have to do in the coming weeks:
• Plan supply shopping (food, tools, building supplies)
• Go on a trip to Dawson City
• Install LED lights and a bigger stove in the house
• Build a new raised garden bed
• Pick more berries
• Finish my garden harvest

Photo (next page): Unidentified, very big mushroom (August 24, 2009)

Lowbush cranberries (August 14, 2010)

One berry leads to another
August 27

At first I picked with the plan to get all the berries in a certain spot before I moved on. Then, one afternoon, I went on an exploratory picking trip, meandering around, stopping only where I found an abundance of berries. The next time I worked on that skill and followed the lead of the berries and my instincts. Unlike highbush cranberries, which are all over the forest clearings and along the waterways, lowbush cranberries are rare around here. Finding and picking them is a challenge. Foraging for and finding those patches of big red cranberries nestled into the moss is exhilarating, almost like gambling!

I am thinking about the philosophical implications of that discovery: Instincts versus analytical planning. It is scary, because if I follow the lead of the berries I can never pick them all, and I never know in advance where I will end up. The bucket generally fills up before all the berries are picked and I have to come back to the studio to empty the bucket usually with the feeling of having left something precious behind.

Bald eagle carving by Gaetan Beaudet (June 6, 2012)

Neighbors migrating
September 3

As the summer comes to an end, our migratory neighbors are heading south, and we are delighted to catch glimpses of timid wildlife: This morning a juvenile bald eagle landed on the top of a spruce tree right in front of our kitchen window.

Flocks of cranes, geese and ducks are moving south as steadily as the river is moving north. Even our human neighbors who spent their summers in the area are gone. The odd moose hunter's boat (the hunting season has started) disturbs the peaceful silence along the river.

First snow on the mountains (September 27, 2009)

This IS Bush Life
September 6

I have been experiencing life out here as a sequence of unavoidable events demanding immediate and creative attention. Up until recently, I was waiting for some mundane everyday life to set in, but it starts to dawn on me that the extraordinary is the rule: The flood in May 2009 might have represented an extreme, but other facts like the mosquitoes that arrive every summer like a plague, the lack of just the right tool or part and the fun of creative improvisation on the job, as well as the extreme temperatures of winter and how they sometimes lock us into the house for weeks at a time keep us company year after year.

And so I come to the preliminary conclusion that bush life is dealing with a series of unforeseeable events that need to be juggled with. We are working on multiple projects at the same time, always improvising on the job and we have to accept imperfection. We never have enough money, are tired and satisfied in the evening, and we experience moments of total freedom and oneness with the world around. Slowly, I came to realize, that no other lifestyle would fulfill me the same.

Shedding leaves

September 13

The forest is in motion. No longer is it quiet. Leaves are rustling, quivering. A breeze, a gust of wind shakes their connection with the tree one more time, before they fall.

Gracefully they sail through the air, golden leaves, red leaves, all sailing down, touching my face gently, breaking up the warm rays of sunlight. When I walk, the leaves underneath my shoes are crunching. When I stop, I hear them rustling and quivering. It is as if a new spirit has entered the forest.

Yellow birch (September 7, 2009)

The flood in May 2009: The water rose another 50 centimeters after this photo had been taken. You are looking at the roof of the old cabin submerged in water (May 2, 2009)

Forest fires, floods and earthquakes
September 18

We felt a series of small tremors last night. Something in the kitchen rattled, and Lance gave a bark. To me the earthquake felt like dizziness, and if it hadn't been for the noises in the kitchen, that is what I would have taken it for.

During breakfast, Gaetan asked me if I had felt the second tremor, too. I affirmed and he remarked casually: "Yeah, we get it all: wild fires, floods and earth quakes"!

The last forest fire struck Poppy Creek in summer 2004. The fire had stopped by our second bridge, about 500 meters from the house.

During the flood in May 2009, the water level rose to an estimated 400-year high. Our old cabin was submerged in ice cold water up to the roof.

Lance does not need a mattress (September 23, 2009)

Minor unevenness
September 23

As I am becoming more and more involved in our life out here, I tend to lose the ability to write about it. I just wrap myself into my little issues and ponder over them. Some days though, a trace of humor overtakes me and I see things with different eyes.

The issue at hand is our mattress. The good thing has been in Gaetan's possession for decades, I dare say. It is a good brand (its likes can still be found in renowned warehouses), latex, and it is perfectly comfortable for ONE person. Over the years it has taken on Gaetan's shape, right in the middle of itself, with a permanent lengthwise indent, several centimeters in depth. What is comfortable for one becomes an issue for two, since both will converge toward the indent, which proves to be a source of nightly disputes. Too many sharp elbows in each other's ribs finally tipped the scale and I changed the mattress. I do not know how good this "new" futon is (we inherited it) and how long it will last.

A new latex mattress, king size, is on my shopping list for next spring. It is not that easy though: What's a basic commodity for people in more populated areas does not come easily out here. It is not easy to find a warehouse that ships big things like mattresses to remote locations, and even if we find one, we have to expect high shipping costs. After long hours of shopping and a painful financial transaction we might have it in Dawson, but then we still have to transport a big thing that must not get wet on the boat. In this spirit, consider yourself lucky, if you have a good mattress!

Dry grass in wet mud, small lake, mountains in the background and the warm sun behind us (September 19, 2010)

Fall impressions
September 23

Quickly, the cold north wind is tearing down the remaining leaves. Within a few days our yellow world will change colors again and soon it will be winter! Already, the weather forecast calls for snow in some areas of the Yukon Territory.

Winter left his business card
September 26

On our latest trip on the river, we experienced the first snow fall accompanied by gusts of cold wind:

We are on the boat, heading downriver. Rain is drizzling. As the boat accelerates, the rain starts to pierce my face. I sit down, protecting my face from the wind. A small flock of ducks is passing at my eye level, followed by a snowflake! Then, another one, a flurry! I stand up, greeting winter. A smile emerges from inside me, plants itself on my face, and won't leave. I face the wind, the snow, winter. I lean into the wind, let it hold me at an angle much smaller than 90 degrees. The clouds are hanging low. We cannot see far ahead. White water crowns the ripples on the river. We come around a bend, gusts of wind rattle the boat. Soon, I get cold and there is nowhere to hide on the boat. Gaetan's eyes are fixed on the water ahead of us.

We were on the river for less than two hours, but the trip seemed to take much longer. How lucky I felt to come back to our warm cabin with a fire cracking in the stove!

Moose tracks in the sand by the river (September 6, 2009)

Moose hunt: An introduction
October 3

Between the onset of night frost in early October, and mid-October, when ice starts to build up on the boat and we have to pull it out of the water, we go moose hunting.

Minutes ago, Gaetan went on his first moose spotting trip, equipped with his binoculars, a thermos with hot coffee and his gun. It is 7:45 in the morning. The day is dawning and a gentle white light with a trace of pink outlines the mountains against the grey sky. Gaetan will go upriver by boat and then drift down, looking for moose. When moose are in rut, they spend more time on the beaches and other open areas, as they pursue the opposite sex and (if they are male) challenge other bulls. Occasionally, Gaetan would stop at an island or a slough and walk around to look for signs of recent moose activity.

As it turns out, the hunter will not see a moose today. Some years it takes weeks of early morning moose spotting trips before Gaetan has a chance to shoot an animal, and some years we do not get one at all.

Shortly before departure in Dawson City: Fully loaded boat and happy crew
(October 8, 2009)

Buying winter supplies in Dawson City

October 9

Last night at 11 pm we arrived home from our last trip to Dawson. We left town as the light of a sunny late fall day was fading and the half moon was rising from the east. The water looked like oil, reflecting the dim light of a day morphing to night. The moon accompanied us with his pale yellow light. Spruce trees along the river were casting longs shadows that reached into the river like fingers reaching from the past into the future.

It was a long three hours on the river, and Gaetan spent every minute in total concentration. Today I picked his brain and here is what he had to say:

"You have to constantly know where you are going. (...) It's not relaxing, that's for sure!"

How do you read the river at night? "You don't, you just know. You know where the sandbars are. You hope that there is no moose swimming in the river or any debris coming down. You can never be sure, but usually there is nothing

Cold morning, some snow, fog, boat partly unloaded, 12 meter high steep bank, and one hand, holding the wire for the winch (October 9, 2009)

this time of the year.

What do you like about night travel on the river? "It's nice with the moon. A little bit of snow on the banks helps to brighten it up so you have a better depth perception".

After a good night's sleep without any noises we were getting ready to unload the boat and store things away, when a snowstorm blew in and blessed us with the first thin layer of fluffy white!

We put the boxes in a sled and used a winch to pull the sled up the steep, 12-meter high bank. From there, we moved everything into the wheelbarrow and I hauled it about 500 meters to the cottage and the studio, where I had started fires to keep the vegetables from freezing. 10 loads with the sled equaled about 50 loads with the wheelbarrow.

Tomorrow, I will start to cut up and freeze more than 10 big boxes of vegetables. It is a good feeling to have all the food we need for a long winter, right at our house. Now, we are practically self-sufficient!

Celery ready to be cut (October 11, 2009)

Processing vegetables
October 12

Vegetables and more: The shopping list I had been preparing all summer had included organic and regular fruit and vegetables, dry and canned food, as well as household items. I buy as much organic and bulk food as I can. It seems unavoidable though that some of it comes a long way. Checking the boxes for their origin, I wonder if there is a way to avoid those long hauls.

Processing vegetables – Day 1: The bananas from Honduras went into the freezer, box and all. Next to them I put the two frozen turkeys from Manitoba, Canada. Then I took on the green peppers, two boxes or 44 pounds. Some of them had soft spots already, but most of them had made the long trip from Fresno, California, undamaged and were still crunchy. I cut about half the peppers and put them in Ziploc bags. Some of them went into vacuum sealed bags. We will keep them into spring, when things start thawing. The rest of the peppers are awaiting immediate consumption or pickling with other crunchy vegetables. In the evening, I wrapped the 50-pound bag of onions into blankets, to keep the bulbs safe from frost.

Processing vegetables – Day 2: Before I had my first cup of coffee, I fed the sourdough starter. Several hours later I kneaded the bread, covered it with a thin layer of vegetable fat, and put it into bread pans. Sourdough bread takes longer to rise than regular yeast bread. It spent the better part of the day in the warm surroundings of the wood stove, before I baked it.

Next, I brought the three boxes of broccoli over to the studio. 60 pounds of broccoli crowns from Salinas, California, awaited processing. Three hours later, I had these vegetables chopped and packed into 28 big Ziploc bags. The

My last garden vegetables: broccoli, cauliflower and kohlrabi (September 24, 2009)

broccoli went into the freezer and I went to the cottage to sort through the box of Gala apples (from Kelowna, British Columbia, Canada). Most of them looked very good. Only a few had started to rot from the inside. Gaetan requested an apple pie.

Processing vegetables – Day 3: Celery was my target vegetable of the day. The more I get used to my chopping routines, the more efficient I get. My celery operation looked quite professional. However, it still took me three hours to fill the 19 4-liter bags.

In the afternoon I baked an apple pie and cut some firewood for the cottage. It feels nice to work with the chainsaw again!

Looking ahead: 24 cauliflowers, 25 pounds of carrots and 80 pounds of cabbage remain to be dealt with, but I need a break. Also, those vegetables are fine for now, and the freezer is working overtime already, putting all the vegetables therein into a frozen state. I will work on the bridge today and clean up around the new house, before the snow covers everything up.

The vegetables and fruits that we do not want to freeze should be in a root cellar. There will be one under the new house - next year. We will need to dig deep into the gravel, and then insulate the bottom and the walls really well. The heat emerging from the heated kitchen will keep the root cellar frost free. Otherwise, everything that is left without a heating source will freeze during the winter. This winter, the onions and their friends (garlic, cabbages, carrots, potatoes, and apples) will have to live with us. The cabin keeps shrinking, it seems.

Moose (October 3, 2010)

Moose hunt
October 18

Moose hunt - Day 1: I was hauling some firewood to the guest cabin when Gaetan spotted several moose on the island out front. He called me and we rushed to the boat. Ten minutes later Lance and I were dropped off at the lower end of the island. While Gaetan landed the boat at the tip of the island, Lance and I walked in the woods, with the sun in our eyes, making noise, hoping that the big mammals would leave the forest where Gaetan could see them. At one point we heard the *to-tonk-to-tonk* of hooves in the sand. Actually, I felt the vibration as much as I heard the sound. A few minutes after that Gaetan broke off the operation. He had seen the animals, two young females. While he had remained motionless at a distance of several hundred meters, they had casually crossed the river in front of him. We went home, happy for the chance to do that drill, but knowing that we were still without meat for the winter.

Moose hunt - Days 2-5: Every morning at dawn, Gaetan went upriver and drifted down, looking for moose. He did not see any though. Other than that we kept monitoring the area along the river as far as we could see from the bank. The only big mammal Gaetan saw was a female caribou (they are not

Sandstorm by the river (October 3, 2010)

only rare but also protected from hunting) on the tip of the island out front.

Moose hunt - Day 6: Gaetan went out again in the early morning. Two hours later he came home and told me that he had gotten a moose. He estimated that the bull had been four to five years old.

We have to butcher the meat right where the animal has died, no matter where that is. Luckily, Gaetan is not only a good and accurate hunter, but is also patient enough to wait for an animal that is close to the river. Another local hunter shot a moose at a lake more than a kilometer from the river. He then had to carry the meat, piece by piece on his back through brush-wood to the beach where he had parked his boat.

Even at the best of times, it takes us about five hours to gut the animal, skin it, cut it up (hind legs, front legs, rib cage cut in half, neck, rump, head with antlers) and haul each piece into the boat, drive home and haul the pieces up the bank, cover them in cotton meat bags and hang them high up in the trees. The meat freezes, and some of the pieces will stay there until late winter. It takes me about eight days to process the meat, one piece at a time in the house.

Trail work
October 19

I cleared some of our wood trail downriver the past two days. The flood had left most of the trees and bushes in a horizontal position. The area was not accessible in the summer because the ground was too swampy. Now that it has been freezing for several days, the trails are accessible for us, and I was in a rush to finish the trail work before snow obscures everything.

Looking across the river (November 27, 2010)

Winter

Silence - Solitude - Artwork
Routines - Darkness

Ice-covered river with recently frozen overflow and sun low in the sky
(December 3, 2009)

First snow (October 24, 2009)

Ice and snow
October 20

The temperature has been dropping. Hardly does it climb above freezing now, and the snow that falls in regular intervals slowly covers the dry, brown and grey ground in a fresh, clean white blanket. Soon, we will be landlocked while the river freezes. Usually in late December we will be able to break a trail to reestablish a physical connection with the rest of the world.

At the high of noon, the sun is still low above the horizon. Soon, we will lose it altogether on our side of the river. For three months, we will be without direct sunlight.

Ice has been building up at the mouth of the creek for days. Two days ago, we spotted the first slush and ice coming down the river. It makes crunching sounds when it is rubbing against the boat and slowly, ice builds up on the outside of the boat. Soon it will be time to pull it out of the water.

Carving birds
October - April

When the hunting season is over and the winter supplies are stored away, it is time for Gaetan to start carving. From October to April, he disappears into his shop for up to six hours per day. He told me once that having those birds around brings perpetual spring into the cabin for him.

When he has decided which bird to carve, he looks for a suitable base, to be able to position the bird correctly. The base consists of a piece of wood that represents a connection to the bird's natural habitat. Gaetan finds his bases – they are usually bent in some unique way – when he goes for walks, or while he is cutting firewood.

Next, he looks for the appropriate self-made pattern. He stores those two-dimensional models in glossy magazines along with descriptions of the birds. Once he finds the right pattern, Gaetan traces it onto a piece of Tupelo, a soft carving wood that grows in the southern parts of the US. With a hand saw (for bigger birds he uses the chain saw) he gives the future bird a rough cut. Most of Gaetan's birds are males, because their plumage is more colorful.

By now, Gaetan has been working on the carving for several hours. At this point, he starts the generator to remove more wood with a power tool. To catch some of the developing dust, he uses an electric air filter. The tools are noisy and Gaetan usually plays loud music from the Gipsy Kings, Alanis Morissette, or the Rolling Stones.

The carver uses his creative breaks to walk to the river bank or pour himself a cup of coffee (the coffee is kept warm on the stove all day). The bird is clearly recognizable as such by now. The generator is off again, since the tools used during this phase can be operated by battery. They look and sound like a dentist's drills. Before he starts carving, Gaetan uses a pencil to outline the feathers on the bird's body. He drills holes for the glass eyes and the metal feet and puts them in place with some putty. He molds the soft material with a pointy tooth pick. But most of the time is spent carving every single visible feather, down to the fine hair! Once that is done the bird is attached to his base. The base itself is mounted on a sanded, stained and varnished birch-wood plate.

When he has some good daylight, Gaetan starts painting his creation. After every coating, the bird is put aside to dry. The artist usually paints several birds at the same time to make efficient use of his resources. It takes five to ten coatings of oil paint (which allows more blending time and does not freeze in the cold season) before a bird is done.

I like the last coatings best. With all the fine accents and dots the carving comes alive! Once the bird is painted, the bottom of the base is signed and dated. The finished bird carving stays in the cabin for a while, until Gaetan is ready to let it go.

Photos (this and following pages):
Carving of a bald eagle, which takes 400 to 500 hours: Tracing the pattern onto the wood, rough cut with a chainsaw, detail work with grinder, carving and painting. The last photos show the finished carving.

Are we stuck in ice?

October 22

We had been planning to go on our last trip of the boating season on Monday morning: On Saturday we had seen the first ice floating down the river. By Sunday, the water surface was covered in ice and slush. On Monday morning things looked a bit better. "Manageable, I have seen worse", said Gaetan. It took him a while to warm up the motors and get the water pumps going. Then I untied the boat and pushed it off the shore while I jumped in. Gaetan put one motor fully into the icy water, and brought it up to speed, but the prop was cavitating. There was not enough water coming toward it, since the ice that had built up on the bottom of the boat was creating some sort of vacuum or disturbance. Consequently, the boat could not gain much speed and it took about 10 minutes to come back 500 meters against the current.

My hopes to go to town one last time before freeze-up and pick up some cheese and the mail fell. We would have to spend two months without cheese. Also, we did not have much moose meat left. We had planned to get some of the frozen meat we store in a friend's freezer in Dawson City.

Gaetan pulled the boat out of the water and took the ice off. The temperature was just below freezing. The ice came off quite easily when he hit the boat with a rubber hammer.

On Tuesday, things looked much better with hardly any ice floating down the river. Apparently, it had been very cold in the southern Yukon a week prior, then it warmed up and the ice that had formed loosened up and was transported downriver. That is what we had seen: A lot of ice coming down for a period of three days, and then the river had been ice-free again. We went to Dawson City on Tuesday morning. Too late I found out that the cheese I had ordered was not in my grocery packages (had I only checked in town!). We will not have cheese on our menu until we can hopefully go shopping again in late December.

The next day, Gaetan started to pull the boat out of the water and store it for the winter.

Photo (next page): Pulling the boat out of the water (October 24, 2010)

Food stash, possibly from gray jays, in an abandoned bird's nest (October 31, 2010)

Watching wildlife on big screen
November 1

Through our big living room window, we are looking at a constantly changing scenery inhabited by the most wondrous creatures: Whenever we are sitting down for breakfast, lunch, or dinner, our wild neighbors are continuing their own business outside. Weasels are bouncing about, grouses are eating berries along the trail, grey jays are stashing and retrieving food, red-polls are flocking all over birches, pine grosbeaks are hanging heavily on highbush cranberry bushes, and squirrels are doing the squirrel thing (keenly observed by Lance). Even a black bear and her cub traveled past our big living room window a while back. All that takes place in front of the magnificent backdrop of snow covered mountain peaks and a river that carries more and more ice every day.

And that is not all: With the freshly fallen snow, we can read up on what the shyer neighbors have been up to. Yesterday, Gaetan found the tracks of a grizzly bear that was (hopefully!) looking for a den, we saw rabbit tracks everywhere, and fox tracks gave that animal's nightly presence away.

A few days ago, the full moon was rising from behind the mountains, casting a street of light across the water. I was sitting in my chair, watching, and I felt very grateful and at peace.

View downriver (October 28, 2011)

Silence around us
November 7

The days are getting shorter. The sun left for the south, packing the red and orange components of her light spectrum, leaving us with the cool colors of winter. The creek is slowly freezing and its happy rippling sounds are getting trapped under the ice.

The river is whispering tiredly, while junks of ice are crushing along the shoreline, slowly building up a rim of ice. More and more ice is moving slower and slower. One day soon, everything will come to a halt, and then the river will be silent, too.

The remaining sounds are muffled by a layer of soft snow. Most birds are gone. Occasionally the carefree chirps of a grosbeak cut through the silence. The grey jays forage for food with less playfulness and more urgency: It is about surviving, finding food, staying warm.

We are blessed with a warm cabin. At eight in the morning it is still dark outside. A snowstorm is blowing, making the minus 12 degrees Celsius feel much colder.

Self-made pair of mukluks (November 18, 2009)

Homemade leather boots
November 14

Our projects are diverse and take our minds off the November twilight. Gaetan is cutting firewood in the mornings and works in his carving studio in the afternoons. I am attending to my household chores in the morning. After a few hours outside I retreat to my indoor project, a pair of insulated leather gloves with a split index finger. Early in the afternoon I have to light an oil lamp to help me see behind my old singer sewing machine. The sewing machine runs on human power and is equipped with a treadle.

I love to walk bare-feet. Since I first wore mukluks at minus 30 degrees, I am an enthusiastic proponent. Walking in leather boots without a rubber sole feels like walking bare feet in the snow! But you have to keep moving, otherwise your feet will cool off from the bottom. Even inside I am wearing a pair of ankle-high leather boots, because I am prone to cold toes. I wear all my leather boots with thick duffel liners and felt insoles.

My appearance north of the feet does not look feminine either: I wear insulated bibs to go outside, and even indoors I wear long underwear and hooded shirts. Not that it is cold inside but I do not want to have to dress up every time I go outside.

The magic of water
November 17

The creek is freezing up, and so is our waterhole. Every day before I dip the bucket into the precious liquid, I have to use the ax and reluctantly destroy the wonderful ice crystals that have grown the night before. Yesterday I brought my camera along and took a few pictures before I swung the ax.

Gaetan says we have to destroy nature's unique creations, in order to sustain our lives. Without water we would be dead within days. That puts things into perspective for me.

Water hole with ice crystals (November 25, 2009)

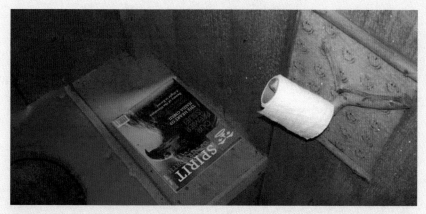

In the winter, the reading material we keep in the outhouse is for display only: Snow has blown in from the side and accumulated behind the magazine (November 28, 2010)

Snow impression
November 20

Yesterday morning we woke to 22 centimeters of fresh snow. It covered everything, including the most delicate twigs. The snow did not provide any resistance, even though we were walking in up to our knees! All morning, we were walking around like on clouds and with little, dreamy-happy smiles on our faces.

In the course of the day, trees shed their loads and clouds of powder fluttered down. It looked like little explosions on weeping branches, followed by a deep sigh of relief of the respective tree.

Outhouse musings
November 29

Most of the time, an outhouse is an uncomplicated and very convenient facility. Even in the summer time, when mosquitoes are searching for exposed skin, a mosquito-coil on the bench right beside the outhouse-user will keep danger at large. But today, at minus 20 degrees Celsius with blowing wind, it feels as drafty in that little place as in the bird feeder. Beautiful big ice crystals are covering the walls and the toilet paper, and for a brief moment I considered an outhouse-free day.

The moral of the story is: Enjoy and appreciate your luxuries, even if they cease to feel precious.

River-ice stopped (December 4, 2010)

Quiet and motionless: River froze!
December 4

December 1. It is cold and the temperature is supposed to drop even more. This morning, we measured minus 30 degrees Celsius. The river sounds really loud with more and more ice pushing down. The ice might stop soon, marking the spot in time we refer to as freeze-up.

We believe that the ice jammed up somewhere not far upriver from our place (there is a spot where a big rock sticks into the middle of the river, forcing the water to make a 90-degree turn – ideal conditions for a jam!), leaving us with an open river, while in places like Dawson City the river froze weeks ago. Luckily, a few days ago, the ice jammed up below Eagle, about 40 kilometers downriver from here. Now, the river is slowly freezing up from there towards upriver. We hope that it will reach our place within the next days. Indicators for it to happen soon are that the water level is rising, the ice is slowing down, and less water vapor is rising from the river.

December 3. The Yukon River at Poppy Creek froze around three in the afternoon. After seven months of seeing all that open water in constant motion and hearing the diverse sounds it makes, the quiet white stillness of the newly

Overflow along the river bank (December 3, 2009)

immobilized ice sheets looks and sounds strange, unusual. We were excited though to be at the shore when the ice jam reached and passed Poppy Creek.

The motionless silence of the river is characteristic for how we experience winter. Except for the grey jay family and the chickadee flock who visit the bird feeder regularly, as well as our local squirrel neighbors who seem to be in motion all the time, our surroundings provide little visual distraction. Consequently and because I need some sort of diversion sometimes, I find myself staring at Gaetan or Lance, as they mosey around the house. Lance does not mind, but Gaetan is not particularly fond of my keen interest in his activities.

Freeze-up also gives us a new sort of freedom: Soon we can start traveling on the river again. In a few weeks, we will be able to check our mail, buy fresh eggs and see other people – after more than two months of seclusion.

Addition: It might sound strange that we are still looking at open water in December at minus 30 degrees Celsius. Here is an explanation that is based on Gaetan's 30 year experience with the river: The Yukon River is 2,000 kilometers long and does not freeze everywhere at the same time, nor does it start freezing from the mouth. When the temperature falls below freezing, ice sheets build up on the water surface. Those sheets are carried along by the current and jam up in narrow and shallow spots of the river, especially when the temperature drops and the water level sinks.

Once a jam exists, the oncoming ice comes to a halt too, and slowly the river freezes upriver from the jam. Downriver, the water might stay open for a longer time, because fewer ice sheets are coming down and with the water still moving, it is not easy for the ice to build up on the surface.

Fire pit with bathhouse in the background (December 9, 2009)

Winter laundry
December 10

Yesterday I did our laundry. The load included bed sheets, so I decided to heat the water on the fire pit, instead of the cabin stove. Our little washing machine cannot be operated at these cold temperatures, since the water would freeze in the drainage pipes.

The venture was quite unique: First I had to shovel the snow off the fire pit, collect dry twigs as fire starters, assemble some split wood and light the fire. Then I went to carry buckets of water from the creek to the fire site. I filled the tub and added the laundry. The wet sheets that were on top of the water quickly froze! At minus 20 degrees Celsius the water vapors were so thick that I could not see my laundry as I was stirring the tub. My bronchi were jubilant! When the water was warm enough, Gaetan helped me to take the tub off the fire and I washed and wrung out the sheets, and then, in a second cycle, rinsed and wrung them out again, before I started a fire in the sauna stove to dry things. The humidity in that little room was soon very high. Entering the sauna felt like being transported to the tropics. Within a few hours my laundry was dry and we had fresh sheets for the night!

Solstice fire at full moon (December 21, 2010)

Winter solstice
December 21

It is dark outside, cold and silent. But the twenty-first day of December marks a turning point: The days are getting longer, lighter, warmer and someday nature's sounds will reawaken.

Every year on December 21, we light a solstice fire by the river bank:

The full moon is rising over snow covered mountains
Its cold light reflecting from sparkling fresh snow
Breathless silence of a cold winter night awaits us
Dog paws are crunching in deep snow
We are gathering around a pile of dry wood
Anticipating warmth
Stiff fingers are igniting a match
Flames start flickering hesitantly
We move closer
Finally feeling the warmth
The flames are consuming the wood
Sparking ancient memories, connecting us
People seeking the warmth of a fire: now, before and after our time

Waterhole in the ice (January 9, 2010)

The art of waterhole maintenance
January 13

It seems normal this time of the year that the temperature drops below minus 40. The creek freezes solid, starting from the mouth, and the water that follows from upstream starts to overflow, escaping its frozen under-ice ways through cracks and openings like my waterhole. First, the water-level rises and the current slows down. Eventually, the water starts to overflow and the hole freezes from the sides and from the top.

To prolong the life of my waterhole, I am building walls around the opening. At first, I used the packed snow I had insulated the plywood with (the plywood had covered the hole). The past four days though the overflow level has been rising 30 centimeters per day and I am leaving the hole uncovered, because the plywood would only freeze solid into the ice. Every morning I chop the ice crust which, after a night at minus 40 degrees is about 10 centimeters thick, and I use the ice chunks to build up a wall around the hole. Then I scoop up the slush and fill the cracks. At this temperature, my liquid mortar freezes quickly. So far I am staying ahead (barely, I admit) of the rising overflow, ice and water levels. Compared to a week ago the ice is now half a meter thicker.

Waterhole exposed to overflow (January 20, 2010)

Gaetan inspected my efforts. I asked him what he considers the most important thing in the art of waterhole maintenance. "Persistence", he proclaimed, "you have to attend to your waterhole every day, as long as you possibly can to postpone the inevitable, because eventually it will freeze. Then you have to move up the creek, looking for a new water hole".

Waterhole update
January 22

The ice at our waterhole is growing thicker and thicker: Two days ago it measured more than a meter. What is a small creek in the summer looks more like an ice-covered pond now, with trees growing in it. Getting water becomes so much more unpredictable and exciting when the natural setting changes daily!

New trail in deep snow (April 3, 2006)

Breaking a trail
January 30

Gaetan, Lance and I have been here by ourselves for two months. In early December, we started to break a trail to Forty Mile, an old village site with road access halfway between here and Dawson City. After about 15 kilometers we ran into a wall of ice: Chunks of ice had piled up on top of each other before they froze into what looks like a giant version of crushed ice floating in a drinking glass that has been put in the freezer.

When the river stopped, the water level had dropped quickly, and the ice along the shore had no time to build up. Now it is not thick enough to drive on. When he broke through with his snowmobile, Gaetan decided that it was time to turn around. But first we had to get his vehicle out! It was stuck, nose first, in a hole that was one meter deep and approximately two by two meters wide. In a backbreaking action we pulled the snowmobile out and turned it around. Who says you won't sweat in the cold!

Going back home was adventurous too, because the lights on my old Bravo did not work and it was getting dark. Several times I hit junks of ice and rocks real hard, with my wrists functioning as shock absorbers. Lance was tired from running in deep snow and I gave him a ride on the seat behind me. He did not like that very much since there was no way for him to brace himself, and he jumped off. When Gaetan gave him a ride, the dog was traveling on his lap. We made it home. All three of us went to bed early.

We were a bit sore the next day. Since it was snowing and the temperature had dropped to minus 20 degrees overnight, we decided to take the day off from trail breaking. As soon as it had warmed up a bit, we wanted to go back to where we had to turn around and start chopping a trail through the ice chunks. Once in Forty Mile, we could most likely travel to Dawson City on the road. Our Christmas mail was awaiting us at the post office – what an incentive to reconnect with civilization!

It took another month before it had warmed up enough for us to be able to go all the way to Forty Mile. First, the temperature had dropped to minus 45 degrees Celsius and stayed there for four weeks. Then, within a few days, it warmed up to plus two degrees. Spontaneously we went on our second trail breaking trip on January 15, which was more successful, although just as exhausting as the first one. We had to chop ice, pull the snowmobiles out of cracks, and manually push them over chunks of ice. When we were in sight of Forty Mile we found that there were three ice sheets that needed to be removed, along with a tree that had blocked the entrance to the boat ramp. Like the time before we came back home at dusk. After five hours on the snowmobile and all that physical workout my knees were stiff and my fingers were frozen.

The next day, we went back and actually made it to Forty Mile. We stayed overnight in a little public cabin by the river. The following morning, we went on to Dawson City. Fortunately, there was a good snowmobile trail on the road (the road is not maintained during the winter months) and we made it to town before dusk.

While the short winter day was coming to an end, we ran our errands. When I entered the grocery store, I was instantly overwhelmed by the warm light-filled room and by the colorful stocked shelves. After all that time in our dimly lit cabin all these new impressions overloaded my sensory system. In the evening, we enjoyed pizza and a shower in a hotel room. After a good breakfast we left town as soon as there was enough daylight to see the trail. With only five hours of daylight, we had to hurry to make it back home before it was too dark to see. During the following days, while we enjoyed our Christmas gifts the winter decided to take a break. It warmed up to plus 4 degrees Celsius. We even got some rain during those four days of premature spring. Then things went back to normal, and we have been enjoying temperatures around minus 20 degrees for the past weeks.

Winter routines
February 6

Out here in the wilderness of the North it seems impossible to get into routines over an extended period of time. In the course of a year we constantly have to adapt our routines to the influences of the natural cycle. The days are short and cold in the winter. In the summer everything is reversed. Food will spoil in the summer, and no ice is available to cool it*, while in the winter everything left outside freezes. If we want to outgrow those restrictions we need to get alternative energy devices like solar panels and water turbines. But even those gadgets are of limited use, because in the winter we do not get any sun for several months, and all waterways are frozen for more than half a year, and in the summer we have an abundance of sun and water, and no way of storing the energy.

That is the big picture. Now to our winter routines: A few days ago I pointed out to Gaetan that there does not seem to be enough time in a day to do everything that I want to do. He confirmed that he shares that notion and told me that he thought people who do not live in the bush do not understand how one can be so busy out here.

I get up at seven o'clock. Gaetan's day has already started up to three hours prior to that. He usually spends his morning hours reading, before he starts to prepare breakfast. My morning routines include reading, writing, eating breakfast, checking emails, knitting and learning French. Everything takes a bit longer because we have less light available, the water is not emerging from a faucet, but has to be hand-scooped from a bucket, and we have to dress warmly when we want to use the toilet.

We do not talk much in the morning. Talking happens as needed and about things of practical nature: What's for breakfast? How cold is it today? Has the dog been out yet? After a cup of coffee it is much more likely that we get into a conversation of more essential nature. Many times we talk about the ways of the mainstream world, and how alienated we feel from them.

Once he has finished his breakfast duties, Gaetan usually takes a walk enjoying the quiet winter world around us. After restocking the firewood supply inside, he disappears inside his carving shop.

As soon as it is light enough I go and get water from the creek. I set out with up to four 20-liter buckets in a sled, a hatchet to chop the ice with, and a plastic pitcher to scoop up the water. The creek has been freezing solid from its mouth and the spot where we can get fresh water has been moving further and further up the creek. Yesterday I saw a snowshoe hare on my way to the precious liquid. Actually I saw it twice. At first sight it took off up the bank, and a minute later it was running zigzag through the forest. If little long-ears had intended to confuse me, a potential predator, he did succeed! When I started to

Photos: Morning routines (April 1, 2009), Gaetan is painting a bird (December 29, 2008), Lance is taking a nap (December 7, 2009)

chop the ice in the spot I had gotten water the day before, the water spurted out like blood from an artery. Water puts a lot of pressure on the ice cover. In some spots the ice cover is bulging up. The creek is full of life and when we get water we have to be careful not to capture those little lobster-like creatures and various insect larvae. I scoop up the water while I marvel at the sounds, the water murmuring, trees cracking, birds such as pine grosbeaks and chickadees feeding and singing in the frozen trees, and Lance foraging for mice with his nose plowing the snow. On my way back down the creek I have to be careful with my load. Sometimes the sled gains speed and slides past me. I might hit bumps and water splashes out of the buckets. At one point I have to carry the buckets up the bank, one by one. We put up a ladder in a 45-degree angle. I can walk on it like on stairs.

Once I have completed my water delivery I go back inside to work on a pair of leather gloves. My old ones are breaking, and producing leather items with a practical purpose is very meaningful to me.

Around noon we eat lunch and after that we go for a walk. It refreshes my mind and body to be out in the cold winter air for a while with no chore to attend to. Yesterday we reached a spot a few kilometers downriver with direct sunlight. After more than two months in the shadows it was so wonderful to feel (or imagine) the sun's warmth on my face again!

We spend the rest of the afternoon in our separate cabins. The dog chooses where he wants to be based on his feeding schedule: Before feeding he stays with Gaetan, because that is where he gets his food, and after that he comes to see me, because I am more likely to let him in and out whenever he wants. All day, Lance is busy eating, sleeping and playing. He loves the big stove in the new house. We are concerned that he might roast himself or catch on fire, since he gets so close to the radiant heat source. Also, Lance leaves his sticks all over the place, preferably on the trails.

Around six o'clock I come back and cook dinner. That, too, takes more time in a household without running water and without electricity. We eat, watch a video, and go to bed.

* We are not using freezers or a fridge in the summer, because in lieu of alternative energy devices, we would have to use a generator all the time, and we do not want that. Our location is not well suited for photo-voltaic panels (we do not have enough sun, because we do not want to cut down too many trees), wind generators (not enough wind), or hydro turbines (there is not enough water in the creek and the river does not have enough downward slope).

Fresh fruit and vegetables
February 10

In the winter, it is risky for us to transport fresh produce, since we do not have road access. The food might freeze, spoil or both on its long way from a faraway grocery store to Poppy Creek. Most food will not survive the cold and bumpy six-hour ride on the bouncing sledge of the snowmobile.

Remains of the penultimate apple (February 10, 2009)

So we decided to abstain from fresh food during the winter months.

As for now we are feeding on the following greens: some potatoes, a handfull of onions, about ten carrots, some garlic, and five red beets. We bought all our winter food supplies last October. Most of the fresh vegetables were cut, bagged and frozen. Some, including twenty pounds of organic apples, has been stored in our living room along the cool outside walls. In early December we ate our last fresh apple, an event I had been anticipating nervously. I dreaded the unavoidable: First I ate one apple a day, then I cut that to half an apple per day (Gaetan got the second half), followed by half an apple every other day. I even painted the penultimate apple's core. And then, despite all the measures I had taken, THE day arrived. I was astonished to find that it was very easy to eat that last apple. As a matter of fact, it did not even taste that good. Had I been weaned off my apple fever, before I ran out of apples? I realized that it had been the idea of living without fresh fruit that had scared me, rather than the fact of living without apples itself.

During the first days after the last apple we ate canned fruit. In addition to that I have been drinking homemade cranberry juice (last fall I spent several weeks gathering highbush cranberries). By now I am used to having some canned fruit every now and then. Besides that I take multivitamins. Gaetan thinks that even that is dispensable. I am not ready yet. The apple core is still sitting on the window sill in the studio, all dried up. We still have enough frozen vegetable, dried beans, and canned tomatoes, mushrooms, etc.

I have learned that eating is not just a necessity, but accompanied by a number of stubborn habits, or even addictions. I am still dreaming vividly about fresh fruit though.

Enjoying the first rays of sunlight (February 4, 2009)

Welcome back Sun!
February 10

For the first time since early November, the sun was back in Poppy Creek yesterday. After more than three months, the first rays of golden light barely made it over the hills in the south. Once again, everything seemed to come back to life! When we close our eyes we can already envision bumble bees, the sound of dripping water and the smell of fresh forest ground.

Sun peaking over the horizon (February 13, 2013)

A load of firewood safely at home (March 12, 2009)

Getting firewood: Learning from mistakes
February 16

There is a lot of potential firewood around: grey wood as well as green trees that were felled by natural forces like wind, spring floods, or soil erosion.

We divide the job as follows: Gaetan cuts down the trees, clears off the branches and cuts the dry wood into 1.5 meter chunks, and the wet wood into stove-size pieces. If part of a tree is suitable for lumber, Gaetan hauls it home on his homemade lumber sled, no matter how long the tree is. If a tree is deemed firewood, I collect the pieces, put them on the sled, tie them down, haul them home and stack them.

Some of the things I find challenging are snowmobiles, firewood, and sleds. After a few easy hauling trips with Gaetan close by, I got stuck with a load of firewood all by myself two days ago. He had warned me that this might happen on the trail I had chosen, since it had been broken the day before and was still very soft. In choosing to take it I ran into my misery with my eyes wide open. That does not sound very intelligent, but the alternative was too scary:

Gaetan breaks a trail in deep snow (April 1, 2009)

A trail leading down to the river over a nearly vertical drop off, two meters down. On top of that, the trail made a sharp right turn on the river bank. Two days before Gaetan had taken the snowmobile down the bank to break a trail and the machine got stuck - nose buried into the snow. I thought, and I still do, that going down there under the prevalent conditions would be fatal for a snowmobile novice like me.

Now, back to my decision: To take my chances with the soft trail was not a difficult decision. When I was done packing my sled, Gaetan came around and doubled my load with the argument that the wood was dry and therefore light. Oh well, I thought, and did not argue - little did I know! While I walked to my snowmobile, Gaetan left with his and was soon inaudible. I set off. As soon as I got onto that new trail, I felt the sled sliding into deep snow. That was not good. The Bravo worked hard, but it did not cover much ground. The preliminary end to my wood haul came seconds later. The snowmobile tracks were digging into soft snow, deeper and deeper. I turned off the motor. I unhooked the sled. I left the load behind and started driving. My mind was spinning. I could not pull the load. I had to dump some. Then what? Maybe I would get stuck again. I seriously thought about giving up. I was stuck. I could come back tomorrow, when the trail was harder.

Gaetan with a load of lumber at the clearing by the river (April 2, 2009)

Excuses! Then I remembered statements from the past like "You cannot do that as a woman". Giving up? Not this time! I would do it my way. By that time I was a third of the way home. I turned around, went back to the sled, passing by the site where I had picked up the firewood and collected a pole. With it, I levered the sled ahead, hooked it onto the snowmobile again, started it - and did not move ahead a single centimeter, but about 30 centimeters down, into soft snow. Again I unhooked the sled and moved the snowmobile ahead. Finally, I dumped half my load, fastened the rest, pushed the sled ahead with the lever, and... It worked and I brought my load home safely.

Lesson learned? I don't know. I still had to go back and get the rest of the firewood, and that steep bank, it was still weighing heavily on me. Which trail would I take? I decided to postpone thinking about the matter for the evening.

The next morning, Gaetan built a snow ramp down that bank. After some serious consideration and inspecting the site I deemed it safe enough to give it a try. Loaded with the firewood I had left behind the day before I went on the winding trail to the high bank. My heart was beating fast and my stomach cramped slightly. I saw the bank. It was too late to stop! The next moment I found myself down on the flat bank by the river. I had slid down like a drop of water on a window.

Gaetan examines a tree and cuts lumber (April 12, 2009)

My first chainsaw (March 12, 2009)

Honey, I got you a chainsaw!
March 12

In the wilderness, there is always a practical aspect to loving gestures, it seems. Gaetan bought me a chainsaw, a Husqvarna 350. It weighs about five kilograms and the bar is 46 centimeters long. I had my first assignment yesterday. Before I began, I got a lecture on safe and efficient chainsaw use. Then I was left to remove the branches and cut the trunk into stove-size pieces. The chainsaw was working well: The chain was spinning smoothly with a soft rattling sound, muffled by my safety helmet, cutting the wood with ease. How deceiving that looked! As if there was no danger in the sharp little knives on the chain. I felt like I was holding a weapon. That thing can go through human flesh as smoothly as it goes through wood. While I like to let my thoughts wander off when I do manual jobs, I stayed attentive on this one the whole time, with a mixture of respect and watchful fear.

Once the cutting was done, Gaetan packed a trunk that was designated as lumber, and left me to pack and haul the firewood. Of course, I got stuck with my load; this time at the exit of the wood trail onto the river bank. We are using a new exit, and apparently we have to connect to the river trail with a sharp right turn. I did not know that, or I expected a nice wide loop, since Gaetan had told me that he had broken a trail. Consequently I went into deep snow and got stuck. After a minute of consideration I unloaded the wood, brought the sled and the snowmobile back onto the hard trail, reloaded it, and restarted the snowmobile. It puffed at me with a black misfiring, as if to tell me that it did not approve of my clumsy driving style.

Being able to use a chainsaw marks another step towards self-sufficiency in the life out here for me.

Last piece of moose meat hanging (March 23, 2009)

Cutting moose meat
March 24

The air spoke of spring. We still measured minus 10 degrees Celsius, but somehow, maybe the humidity was higher, it felt like it was warming up.

It was time to work on our moose meat again. We had kept all four moose legs hanging on an appliance (made of poles and boards) high up in the trees, since the meat preserves easily this way in the winter. Over the past six months, we had taken down and processed most of the meat. Now it was time to tackle the last piece. Gaetan took it down and, with a handsaw he cut off a big piece of approximately 10 kilograms. When it is thawed (which could take days), I will cut it up into stir fry chunks and grind the rest.

First family photo: Anya, Manuela and Gaetan (June 27, 2011)

Epilogue: More life in the wilderness
May 2013

Our life took a new turn with our daughter Anya's birth in June 2011. Gaetan took on most of my outdoor chores and my leather projects came to a temporary halt. Anya has been growing a lot over those past two years and is now helping me with some of my chores: She enjoys garden work and sorting through stored vegetables and canned food items. She also loves to play in her sandbox or take a bath in the plastic tub on the porch on a hot summer afternoon.

I am working on another book about our life in the wilderness, now with a child.

We can be reached at <zeitlhofer_manuela@yahoo.ca>

Anya and Papa Gaetan (December 4, 2011)

Anya helping with the firewood
(January 14, 2013)

Anya getting water from the creek
(February 11, 2013)

Anya - simply cute (February 8, 2013)

Snowmobile trip (March 17, 2013)

Summer trip (June 20, 2013)

31611793R00058

Made in the USA
Charleston, SC
22 July 2014